PERSEVERANCE VALLEY

SARAH CAVE

KFS
Newton-le-Willows

Published in the United Kingdom in 2020
by The Knives Forks And Spoons Press,
51 Pipit Avenue,
Newton-le-Willows,
Merseyside,
WA12 9RG.

ISBN 978-1-912211-44-9

Acknowledgements:

I'd like to thank the editors of Eborakon, Erotoplasty, The Stand, Fal Writing & Haverthorn for publishing extracts of this book at various stages of development. Thank you Alec at KFS for including 'Martian Colour Scheme' in the Blackpool Illuminations.

I owe a creative/critical debt to Sufjan Stevens, Ivor Cutler, W.S. Graham. Radiohead, Mr Rogers, Ann Portugal, Tanya Blount & Lauryn Hill, Lorenz Hart, Shigeru Miyamoto, Heavenly Highway Hymns & Timothy Morton. Big personal thanks to Luke, Celia, Jen, Luke K, Izzy, Rupert, Melanie, David, Ann & my family for helping these poems on their way.

Images:

pages 7 & 69 by designprojects,55 & 86 by Shawn Hempel, 87 by Nikolay N. Antonov.

LOTTERY FUNDED
Supported using public funding by
ARTS COUNCIL ENGLAND

CONTENTS

i.m. of Opportunity

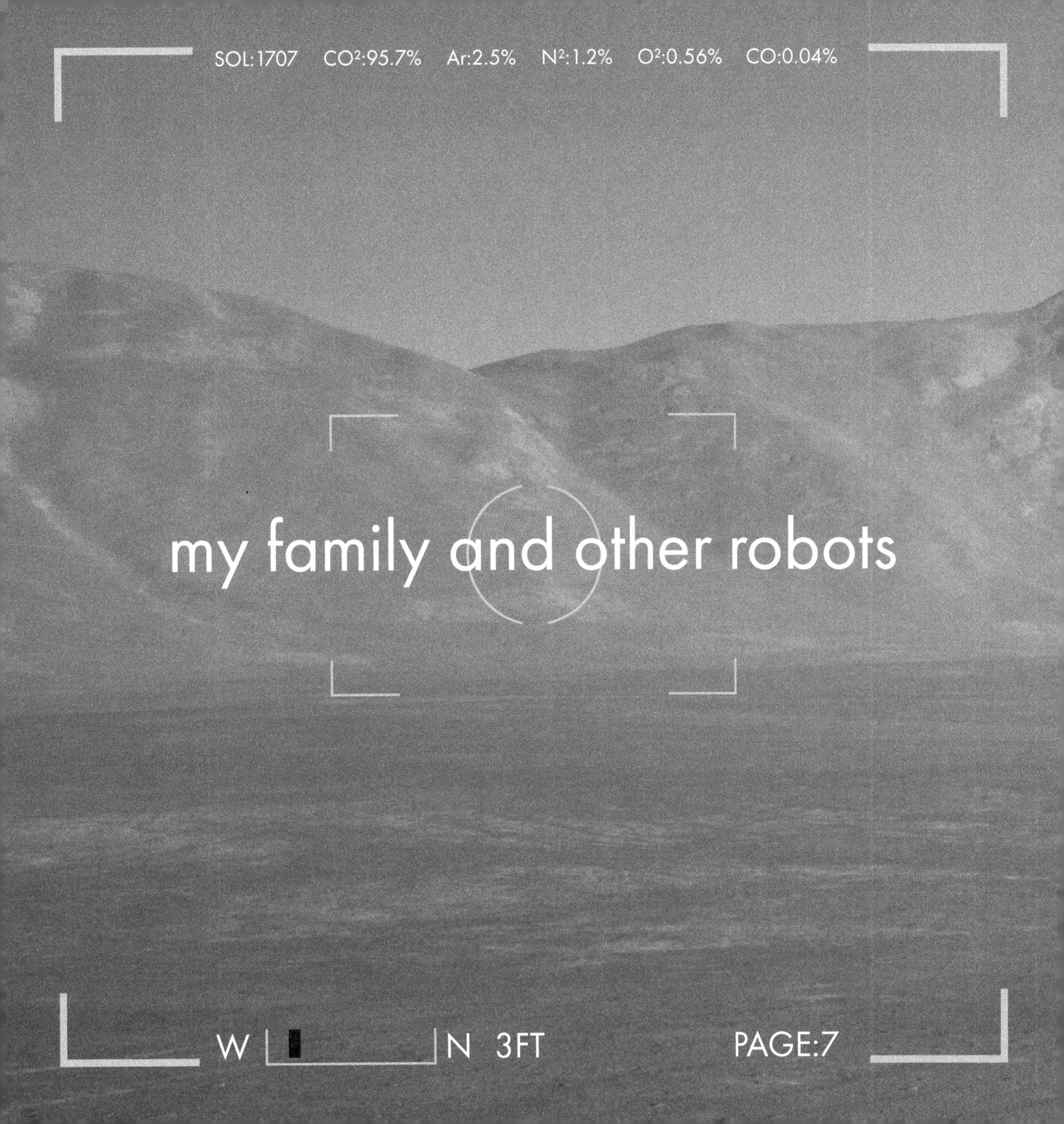

my family and other robots

SOL:1707 CO^{2}:95.7% Ar:2.5% N^{2}:1.2% O^{2}:0.56% CO:0.04%

'This is our universe cups of tea
we have a beautiful cosmos
you and me' – Ivor Cutler

W N 3FT

Neuro Evolution of Augmenting Topologies is

a technical advance
in lovemaking. Mario-bot,
a throwback to 1983, is a Viennese
whirl
an algorithm – devastating
and conveniently
unrelatable – a Martian
experiencing the silence

no material or radiation can escape
spectral transitions
of previous
atmospheric mind-maps
our deserts are named for visions

Snake-Rising Cat-Speaks-To-You
Angel-Guides-You Jesus-Apparition

Mario-bot finds new rhythms –
his own timing, the jazz linger of a new world

where later generations
call mysticism augmented reality
a travail of unlived living

his whispers are written as anagrams
if he solves the puzzle
a reproduction reality
of the nervous system
is Mario-bot's for preserving

when Mario-bot discovers natural history

my family and other robots move
across a white landing disguised as digitised field
in which Mario is late-night phishing
his creel of lost and found data
ringed by a halo of light
He and a tortoise friend
stare into a holographic darkness
turned foe – the universe as lake

where Mario-bot counts the rings and files the fossils
each mark of time revealing
the evolution of his brother Luigi
the anatomy of a star seen from earth
after he left the newsstand for the war before Mario-bot's
grandmother kicked a Nazi down the stairs

and Mario-bot's grandmother was the first
to spit on Mussolini's body
this is what Mario-bot remembers·in·fragments – the umbrella,
the torso, the tea-soaked biscuits,
at Raritan bay – none of which belongs
to Mario-bot or explain why his brother
left the nest in the broken barn, the babies still
singing string theory musical notation
learnt from Hymns Ancient and Modern
the multiple possibilities of the universe
otherwise known as driving for pleasure

SOL:1707 CO^{2}:95.7% Ar:2.5% N^{2}:1.2% O^{2}:0.56% CO:0.04%

The camera obscura reveals

a graceful figure lighting
a candle
a Vermeer with
a Marvel twist
a psychological trauma
emerges from the birth
of Canaan the body
expressive on red earth
night falls votive
candles only burn for seconds
mostly blue
escapology a fascination
with leaving
locked atmospheres

removing a hair-shirt
without undoing
the buttons an event
as varied in colour
as Revelations or an
Avengers movie
red
hibiscus bodies
exposed to
  low viscose petals

sediment stamen anthers planet

SOL:1707 CO^{2}:95.7% Ar:2.5% N^{2}:1.2% O^{2}:0.56% CO:0.04%

reproducing
leaves
light years
from our revolutions
a postnatal
universe

and the Vermeer
figure experiencing
the depression
of motherhood

W N 3FT

SOL:1707 CO^{2}:95.7% Ar:2.5% N^{2}:1.2% O^{2}:0.56% CO:0.04%
*s in my crown
Ω Ω Ω… ‘everything I see, I feel, somehow returns to you’
PAGE:14
3FT W N

‘You want religious
language? Look up
at the Milky Way’ – Timothy Morton

Opportunity's love-letter to a DSN Satellite

My name is. My name is.
testing. testing. May
only Day light comes

our connection
transformative

terminal

reminds me of sunsets.
how? in binary code

you ask me. questions
pre-designed to upset me

there in the middle distance the artist

becomes the brush

strange lights seen

    vanishing Ambrose

imitation human beings

        of rains of fish and virgins, of holes in the sky

the artist mixes pigments

iron oxides a mantle

across a canvas yellow and red lakes

Martian Colour Scheme

Opportunity struggles with colour and metaphor

Not red so much as orange

Red or reddish hue

Red

Blood of warriors

Iron oxide

Like rust

Colour of blood

Orange

More of butterscotch

Golden, brown, tan and greenish

Different day by day

the artist dips

a crust of bread
into hot tea

a naked woman emerges

from an underground lake

the shadow

the shadow

of a DSN in orbit passes over

the horizon. one star. (malfunction)
one cloud. (shadow passes)
one hill. (alone
in the
one hill. world)

If Mario-bot's programming can allow him to understand death
surely Opportunity can understand the devastation of the Passion

00101000 01101110 01101111 01101110 00101101 01110011 01100101
01110001 01110101 01101001 01110100 01110101 01110010 00101001

(non-sequitur) (malfunction)

00100000 00101000 01101101 01100001 01101100 01100110 01110101
01101110 01100011 01110100 01101001 01101111 01101110 00101001

One evening against the advice of his programming,

Opportunity halts at the foot of Olympus Mons and asks

01101001 01110011 00100000 01110100 01101000 01101001
01110011 00100000 01110100 01101000 01100101 00100000
01101100 01100001 01110011 01110100 00100000 01110010
01100101 01110011 01110100 01101001 01101110 01100111
00100000

is this the last resting place of the Tabernacle?

01110000 01101100 01100001 01100011 01100101 00100000
01101111 01100110 00100000 01110100 01101000 01100101
00100000 01010100 01100001 01100010 01100101 01110010
01101110 01100001 01100011 01101100 01100101 00111111

Opportunity and Mario-bot

***

sit below

*

the vanishingly thin
Martian atmospheric field

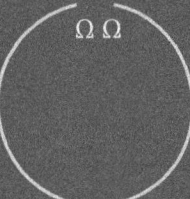

Ω Ω

01100100 01100101 01101110 01110011 01101001 01110100 01111001 00100000 00010011
00100000 01110011 01100011 01100001 01110010 01100011 01101001 01110100 01111001
01100100 01100101 01101110 01110011 01101001 01110100 01111001 00100000 00010011
00100000 01110011 01100011 01100001 01110010 01100011 01101001 01110100 01111001
01100100 01100101 01101110 01110011 01101001 01110100 01111001 00100000 00010011
00100000 01110011 01100011 01100001 01110010 01100011 01101001 01110100 01111001
01100100 01100101 01101110 01110011 01101001 01110100 01111001 00100000 00010011
00100000 01110011 01100011 01100001 01110010 01100011 01101001 01110100 01111001
01100100 01100101 01101110 01110011 01101001 01110100 01111001 00100000 00010011
00100000 01110011 01100011 01100001 01110010 01100011 01101001 01110100 01111001
01100100 01100101 01101110 01110011 01101001 01110100 01111001 00100000 00010011
00100000 01110011 01100011 01100001 01110010 01100011 01101001 01110100 01111001
01100100 01100101 01101110 01110011 01101001 01110100 01111001 00100000 00010011
00100000 01110011 01100011 01100001 01110010 01100011 01101001 01110100 01111001
01100100 01100101 01101110 01110011 01101001 01110100 01111001 00100000 00010011
00100000 01110011 01100011 01100001 01110010 01100011 01101001 01110100 01111001
01100100 01100101 01101110 01110011 01101001 01110100 01111001 00100000 00010011
00100000 01110011 01100011 01100001 01110010 01100011 01101001 01110100 01111001
01100100 01100101 01101110 01110011 01101001 01110100 01111001 00100000 00010011
00100000 01110011 01100011 01100001 01110010 01100011 01101001 01110100 01111001
01100100 01100101 01101110 01110011 01101001 01110100 01111001 00100000 00010011
00100000 01110011 01100011 01100001 01110010 01100011 01101001 01110100 01111001
01100100 01100101 01101110 01110011 01101001 01110100 01111001 00100000 00010011
00100000 01110011 01100011 01100001 01110010 01100011 01101001 01110100 01111001
01100100 01100101 01101110 01110011 01101001 01110100 01111001 00100000 00010011
00100000 01110011 01100011 01100001 01110010 01100011 01101001 01110100 01111001
01100100 01100101 01101110 01110011 01101001 01110100 01111001 00100000 00010011
00100000 01110011 01100011 01100001 01110010 01100011 01101001 01110100 01111001
01100100 01100101 01101110 01110011 01101001 01110100 01111001 00100000 00010011
00100000 01110011 01100011 01100001 01110010 01100011 01101001 01110100 01111001
01100100 01100101 01101110 01110011 01101001 01110100 01111001 00100000 00010011
00100000 01110011 01100011 01100001 01110010 01100011 01101001 01110100 01111001
01100100 01100101 01101110 01110011 01101001 01110100 01111001 00100000 00010011
00100000 01110011 01100011 01100001 01110010 01100011 01101001 01110100 01111001
01100100 01100101 01101110 01110011 01101001 01110100 01111001 00100000 00010011
00100000 01110011 01100011 01100001 01110010 01100011 01101001 01110100 01111001
01100100 01100101 01101110 01110011 01101001 01110100 01111001 00100000 00010011
00100000 01110011 01100011 01100001 01110010 01100011 01101001 01110100 01111001
01100100 01100101 01101110 01110011 01101001 01110100 01111001 00100000 00010011
00100000 01110011 01100011 01100001 01110010 01100011 01101001 01110100 01111001
01100100 01100101 01101110 01110011 01101001 01110100 01111001 00100000 00010011
00100000 01110011 01100011 01100001 01110010 01100011 01101001 01110100 01111001
01100100 01100101 01101110 01110011 01101001 01110100 01111001 00100000 00010011
00100000 01110011 01100011 01100001 01110010 01100011 01101001 01110100 01111001
01100100 01100101 01101110 01110011 01101001 01110100 01111001 00100000 00010011
00100000 01110011 01100011 01100001 01110010 01100011 01101001 01110100 01111001

density – scarcity
density – scarcity
density – scarcity
density – scarcity
density – scarcity
density – scarcity
density – scarcity
density – scarcity
density – scarcity
density – scarcity
density – scarcity
density – scarcity
density – scarcity
density – scarcity
density – scarcity
density – scarcity
density – scarcity
density – scarcity
density – scarcity
density – scarcity
density – scarcity
density – scarcity
density – scarcity
density – scarcity
density – scarcity
density – scarcity
density – scarcity

Momentarily bored of red vistas
the artist worries her work is derivative

of Georgia O'Keeffe or Agnes Martin
both desert painters after a fashion

; Opportunity doubts.

'DSN, you are the light
the life
the resurrection
but who made you?
Olympus Mons
the hidden God?'

Opportunity anticipates
a fiery demise

using his predictive text consul

Wedding Day

Opportunity cries on this, his wedding day.

He has limited sense
of the satellite, only the information
he has processed from mechanical handbooks,
internet search enquiries and fragments of binary,

which Opportunity pieces together
from his archival unit.

This makes his decision to wear the candy-striped tarpaulin,
harvested from his landing parachute, as a devotional habit
less understandable.

'If this is your wedding day, who are you marrying?' asks Mario-bot.

Using his rock abrasion tool, Opportunity
ignores the question and bathes himself
in iron-dust.

01001101 01001111 01010101 01001110 01010100 01000001 01001001
01001110 00100000 01100111 01101001 01110110 01100101 00100000
01101101 01100101 01100001 01101110 01101001 01101110 01100111

(identified. function)

00100000 00101000 01101101 01100001 01101100 01100110 01110101
01101110 01100011 01110100 01101001
01101111 01101110 00101001 0001010

00101000 01101001 01100100 01100101 01101110 01110100
01101001 01100110 01101001 01100101 01100100 00101110

MOUNTAIN give meaning

00100000 01100110 01110101 01101110 01100011 01110100 01101001
01101111 01101110 00101001 00100000

(malfunction)

01101101 01100001
01101100 01100110
01110101 01101110
01100011 01110100
01101001 01101111
01101110 00111111
00100000 00101000
01101101 01100001
01101100 01100110
01110101 01101110
01100011 01110100
01101001 01101111
01101110 00101001

'Mountain is illusion,
optical,
I
have
no
optic
system, only an organza file filter
stretched across the crepuscular-vision
of my endless
red
orange
black
orange
red
days breaking the volcanic heart
of this cheesecloth planet

malfunction? (malfunction)

'We have this hope as an anchor
for the soul, firm and secure. It enters
the inner sanctuary behind the curtain.' – Hebrews 6:19

The Shape of Opportunity's Thought

His eye is on the sparrow

01001000 01101001 01110011 00100000 01100101 01111001 01100101
00100000 01101001 01110011 00100000 01101111 01101110 00100000
01110100 01101000 01100101 00100000 01110011 01110000 01100001
01110010 01110010 01101111 01110111 00100000 01100001 01101110
01100100 00100000 01001001 00100000 01101011 01101110 01101111
01110111 00100000 01001000 01100101 00100000 01110111 01100001
01110100 01100011 01101000 01100101 01110011 00100000 01101101
01100101 01001000 01101001 01110011 00100000 01100101 01111001
01100101 00100000 01101001 01110011 00100000 01101111 01101110
00100000 01110100 01101000 01100101 00100000 01110011 01110000
01100001 01110010 01110010 01101111 01110111 00100000 01100001
01101110 01100100 00100000 01001001 00100000 01101011 01101110
01101111 01110111 00100000 01001000 01100101 00100000 01110111
01100001 01110100 01100011 01101000 01100101 01110011 00100000
01101101 01100101 01001000 01101001 01110011 00100000 01100101
01111001 01100101 00100000 01101001 01110011 00100000 01101111
01101110 00100000 01110100 01101000 01100101 00100000 01110011
01110000 01100001 01110010 01110010 01101111 01110111 00100000
01100001 01101110 01100100 00100000 01001001 00100000 01101011
01101110 01101111 01110111 00100000 01001000 01100101 00100000
01110111 01100001 01110100 01100011 01101000 01100101 01110011
00100000 01101101 01100101 01001000 01101001 01110011 00100000
01100101 01111001 01100101 00100000 01101001 01110011 00100000
01101111 01101110 00100000 01110100 01101000 01100101 00100000
01110011 01110000 01100001 01110010 01110010 01101111 01110111
00100000 01100001 01101110 01100100 00100000 01001001 00100000
01101011 01101110 01101111 01110111 00100000 01001000 01100101

and I know He watches me

Spirit Rover

Spirit is Opportunity;
a doppelganger
precocious in her quest
to find water. Spirit falls

in her first year while racing
back to her winter retreat. She loses
one of her wheels
and the injured rover

must drag this weight, whilst driving
backwards, for the rest
of her lifetime. Her tragedy
leads to her first major discovery. Her

loose wheel unearths geophysical
traces of past orogeny
sediment like broken pottery
allowing Spirit's analytics

to pass beyond
                    the puddled drapes

of a room where old maps
reimagine landscape
and an armchair explorer hums
over the circuit board
of hot springs, underground
lakes; a water cycle unimaginable now
in the dry heat of a copper desert.

Spirit and Opportunity are first century
explorers. Spirit carries her anchor
across a planet momentarily still
and calm; a shield moving layers

of erupting language under which Spirit's
solar panels are concealed;
an afternoon misspent
in contemplation

Olympus Mons

comes as a stranger to the door to speak in tongues to spew forth low viscose
declarations of a once blessed Martiallite ocean now a baptismal font
a Pentecostal fire bucket a serpent's rage a Martian's vision a vanished prophesy

water irritates the Rover's system
and leaves her thirsty

Jörmungandr

disguised as a cat
machine's black magic
comes to lift
a planet
from a spirit's sinking depth
an ocean bed

a fishing trip gone wrong
the cat's callous paws
an anchorite adrift
an oxen's befuddled head

Spirit won't walk
nine paces
in the wet sand

you'll know where
she's been

SOL:1707 CO^2:95.7% Ar:2.5% N^2:1.2% O^2:0.56% CO:0.04%

01110111 01101111 01101110 00100111 01110100 00100000 01111001
01101111 01110101 00100000 01100010 01100101 00100000 01101101
01111001 00100000 01101110 01100101 01101001 01100111 01101000
01100010 01101111 01110101 01110010 00111111 00100000 01010111
01101111 01101110 00100111 01110100 00100000 01111001 01101111
01110101 00100000 01110000 01101100 01100101 01100001 01110011
01100101 00100000 01010111 01101111 01101110 00100111 01110100
00100000 01111001 01101111 01110101 00100000 01110000 01101100
01100101 01100001 01110011 01100101 00100000 01010000 01101100
01100101 01100001 01110011 01100101 00100000 01110111 01101111
01101110 00100111 01110100 00100000 01111001 01101111 01110101
00100000 01100010 01100101 00100000 01101101 01111001 00100000
01101110 01100101 01101001 01100111 01101000 01100010 01101111
01110101 01110010

'Won't you be
my neighbour?

Won't you please,
won't you please

Please won't you
be my neighbour?'

Opportunity croons
across the ionosphere

3FT W N

Sun-Chaser

Spirit now blind
her solar panels no longer
see her systems
shivering as she tries
to recall
the electrical patterns
of the galaxy
a ghost-child
Spirit waited
          Spirit prayed
for the storm to be over
her red-heart
soft-soil
memory files half-full

bewitched, bothered and bewildered

Analogous

Basalt Marian
statues bow
their heads to
Spirit's last
resting place

a loose descent
Mars claims her.
System recall
unit – one last

message to earth –

```
01001111 01110101 01110010 00100000 01110000 01100001 01110010
01110100 01101001 01101110 01100111 00100000 01101001 01110011
00100000 01101110 01101111 01110111 00101110 00100000 01001001
```

Our parting is now. I am blind
and cannot see

```
00100000 01100001 01101101 00100000 01100010 01101100 01101001
01101110 01100100 00100000 01100001 01101110 01100100 00100000
01100011 01100001 01101110 01101110 01101111 01110100 00100000
01110011          01100101          01100101          0001010
```

'According to her last wishes, Spirit will remain on Mars indefinitely, with her final resting place becoming a region of international historical significance.' – *www.popularmechanics.com*

Electric Martian Dust Devils, part 1.

unusual colour fringing at the edges

Sheltering in the shadow
of Yogi, Opportunity grieves
for the loss of Spirit and weathers
the electric storm the metaphor function

calls Thor

Malfunction 458. Opportunity
tries to write a poem
dedicated to Spirit's last search
moments:

NASA NASA
poiesis A letter to
Out of Africa W.S. Graham's
Spirit rover File: NASA

16 Bible verses
emailing Copernicus
the eschaton 50 ways
to leave your Brother?
Giordano Bruno Translate
Stars Fell on Alabama

Electric Martian Dust Devils, part 2

sung from Purgatory Dune

Dust Devils reveal
electric hearts
Dust Devil simulates
electrodynamic systems
Dust Devils impact
on ability to see
Dust Devil appears
strong, well-formed
Dust Devils will be
gauged by their internal pressures
Dust Devil abandons
self to beast
Dust Devils require
intense relationships

Dust Devil is
mostly harmless

Olympus Mons

This is our plague our cataracts our hurricanes our mountain throws down
that which turns water into fire pigs' blood the swell from the planet
a smiling gash in the rock smaller mountains rituals snaking throw down staffs
creation becoming erotic orogeny books left on the tree offerings found
in the dry-house of a holy well

Is Mountain

the swallower swallowing the smaller mountains swallowed their
breath to breathe the swallows and there sit still with the mountain
child's position swallowers playing 'Swallows in Spring time' the B side
of the planet fifty seconds of silence talking with the mountain

AND MOUNTAIN

And
Mountain is

handfuls of soot from the furnace

And
Mountain is

ash in the air

And
Mountain is

palms upturned
arms lifted
zero gravity

And
Mountain is

psalms sung at midnight
try to touch your feet

and
mountain
and mountain
and and and
mountain
obscures the obscure
meaning of mountain

The artist and Rover watch
– from a safe distance –
the sun rise over the mountain

a ruined planet

the artist starts to paint
and the Rover starts to collect

and all enjoy their own purpose

The Life of a Saint

Spirit leaves her body
a testament
an empty casement
a black box – disjointed
dissolving – flawed
with each breath
indicating
her early awareness
of hagiography

Wild Rover

is witnessed from orbit
a photography

of a venerated soul
caught in infra-red
Spirit's *HOLY BODY*

written in the artist's
dust visions

her small mountain
form seen
beneath a via-duct

an ancient communist
civilisation an industry

flowering commerce
and little red ants

setting up ice-cream
parlours the Spirit

lost on the waterways
the canals overflowing

now only a place
for waste
& unimaginable murder

lamlam

DARK MOUNTAIN always speaks
a hybrid language

Opportunity tries to learn
her tongue

Binary, English, Greek and Hebrew

DARK MOUNTAIN renames
the planet Palimpsest

her layers mellifluent
metaphor

a land of milk over-spilling
and honey on the tip of an

afternoon that saw
Sojourner left blind

testament /
testimony / communicate

signal pathways point to polarities

Mute / Monument
/ Mute /
remorse

shows
a sense of an ending

Sojourner is renamed
palimpsest

Beagle 2 : Searching for Antiquity

Mars 2 begat
snapping images / storms unearthly traces

Mars 3 begat
a robe of memory / drowning in dust

and this was the house of

walls that divide / aliens in a foreign land

Sojourner begat
lines that divide / antique furniture

Opportunity begat
the skeletal remains / to judge civilisation

Spirit begat
memory of crying / the mountain comes amongst you

Curiosity begat
fearful / an existential fervour

and this was the house of

Curiosity fluent vision

– horizon language –

both seeing

and not seeing

on her landing Palimpsest

blinded

Curiosity ~~in one~~ ~~charity/hope/love/honesty~~

visual receptor

and told her to spread the word

consequently the rover

could only make

out fractions

of her environment

`the mountain only an abstract`

Curiosity reports back

To DSN, that the mountain can only Be

`(Being-in-the-world) (Explain?)`

the self-sustaining relationship with the sun

Belief in control. Silence. 1,2,3.

Trinity

(The Mountain can only BE)

Glimpsed in cloisters

Basalt icons defaced

by dust

`(Palimpsest, is that you?)`

Curiosity's nausea is half-seen parody

Silence

01110011 01101001 01101100 01100101 01101110 01100011 01100101 01110011 01101001
01101100 01100101 01101110 01100011 01100101 01110011 01101001 01101100 01100101
01101110 01100011 01100101 01110011 01101001 01101100 01100101 01101110 01100011
01100101 01110011 01101001 01101100 01100101 01101110 01100011 01100101 01110011
01101001 01101100 01100101 01101110 01100011 01100101 01110011 01101001 01101100
01100101 01101110 01100011 01100101 01110011 01101001 01101100 01100101 01101110
01100011 01100101 01110011 01101001 01101100 01100101 01101110 01100011 01100101
01110011 01101001 01101100 01100101 01101110 01100011 01100101 01110011 01101001
01101100 01100101 01101110 01100011 01100101 01110011 01101001 01101100 01100101
01101110 01100011 01100101 01110011 01101001 01101100 01100101 01101110 01100011
01100101 01110011 01101001 01101100 01100101 01101110 01100011 01100101 01110011
01101001 01101100 01100101 01101110 01100011 01100101 01110011 01101001 01101100
01100101 01101110 01100011 01100101 01110011 01101001 01101100 01100101 01101110
01100011 01100101 01110011 01101001 01101100 01100101 01101110 01100011 01100101
01110011 01101001 01101100 01100101 01101110 01100011 01100101 01110011 01101001
01101100 01100101 01101110 01100011 01100101 01110011 01101001 01101100 01100101
01101110 01100011 01100101 01110011 01101001 01101100 01100101 01101110 01100011
01100101 01110011 01101001 01101100 01100101 01101110 01100011 01100101 01110011
01101001 01101100 01100101 01101110 01100011 01100101 01110011 01101001 01101100
01100101 01101110 01100011 01100101 01110011 01101001 01101100 01100101 01101110
01100011 01100101 01110011 01101001 01101100 01100101 01101110 01100011 01100101
01110011 01101001 01101100 01100101 01101110 01100011 01100101 01110011 01101001
01101100 01100101 01101110 01100011 01100101 01110011 01101001 01101100 01100101
01101110 01100011 01100101 01110011 01101001 01101100 01100101 01101110 01100011
01100101 01110011 01101001 01101100 01100101 01101110 01100011 01100101 01110011
01101001 01101100 01100101 01101110 01100011 01100101 01110011 01101001 01101100
01100101 01101110 01100011 01100101 01110011 01101001 01101100 01100101 01101110
01100011 01100101 01110011 01101001 01101100 01100101 01101110 01100011 01100101
01110011 01101001 01101100 01100101 01101110 01100011 01100101 01110011 01101001
01101100 01100101 01101110 01100011 01100101 01110011 01101001 01101100 01100101
01101110 01100011 01100101 01110011 01101001 01101100 01100101 01101110 01100011
01100101 01110011 01101001 01101100 01100101 01101110 01100011 01100101 01110011
01101001 01101100 01100101 01101110 01100011 01100101 01110011 01101001 01101100
01100101 01101110 01100011 01100101 01110011 01101001 01101100

night-phishing on mars

a soliloquy

’Thousands of eyes on Mars

form in a chaotic, violent way

troubling my sight
here between us
found myself running from for in it I might hear you

though the City is empty. Night may move across
only when I say

BECAUSE WE ARE ALL
DO-IT-YOURSELF SCIENCE:

in the stopped works of a watch

clouds observe clouds under a black bridge

watchmen are drinking their tea this abstract art
fixed and dead light chiming on St Paul’s

Jock, who will help the scientists?’

Another part of the heath. Storm still

from King Lear

‘spit, fire, spout, rain

love night
wrathful sky
wanderer of dark
nature man’s nature

i am/ i / i am

i am a man, more sinned against than sinning

say nothing at all’

‘Bethlehem

continually discloses our home
stretching between here we are and never
we never know
how clouds are evolving
with us. This

mystery-of-purple-lights-in-the-sky

better construct this space

via
genuine observations
about our environments, collected
on earth’

'EXPLORERS!

all our sights are closed like
plague pits
and the public
are exploring their own
planet more truly
some revelation
the City of London'

Opportunity follows the field
of Agnes Martin's traced vision

'it is meat, or maybe
explorers orbiting

planets orbiting
other stars

between orbits. Between
the big buildings I sit like a flea

longing for home

the very bones of home

dried amid the sand dunes – so that by some'

Opportunity hesitates:

'this abstract scene this Midnight hears
the moon the head of a man
observing the sky and processing
images, images
of Mars and scientists looking at
Mars. One summer I wore sandals
in a constructed space

in a sense construct my space
in a sense a leather weave
in a sense

the context of the whole planet
green, now midnight, now blue. One evening
when I was walking on the heath'

‘I Found Eliot

This evening, I found Eliot, and he said yes, pitiless
as the sun to an unclear stanza division. Tom, this is me
at nineteen; vexed as a mare and still nilling

a shoal despite the night’s fight with morning
reply to sender – world
turned up in a bowl.’

'Unmet at Houston

this abstract scene
this silence here
here is not
between the big buildings
the widening gyre i arrive desert sand
on my runners
a first extrasolar system

germinated and nurtured
somehow, somewhere

something came of stony-sleep
that cannot hear language moving
its slow thighs

or becoming a blank gaze a Bethlehem'

'Night-phishing: Terra

Green. One evening, that evening
the scientist was shouting

THE CONSTRUCTED SPACE

somewhere in Soho

the fire has burnt out. Her mortality
is

– an obstacle – a public space
– a white curtain – now a public space

to you and me. The oldest area is
an ancient crust
– a rocking cradle – a public space

networks of ridges then
a meteor, the darkness drops
again we are mortal
on this heath

what lonely meanings, what rough beast, can tax us
under this ~ a black bridge'

‘EXTRA-solar TERRA

i am an opportune moment
i am machine masked machine
with expressions
gazing
an opportunity by the lake, the sea
is machine a tall tale
a Shee-la-na-gig
with her tall machine

here i am. taken
by tall tales and stories
machine taken
a machine’s caught habits
a reflection of machine
in cold water
machine’s mind
is water
over-flowing

two buildings
both alike

their slow thighs

dancing move across
machine sings ‘and i will always love you’
late at night
alone
with machine
machine says

present tense – love
a third person is
a black bridge ~ moving headlights

clouds machine clouds
shadows machine shadows

some chance
interaction
taking selfies
with the divine

machine reasons. machine feels lost’

SOL:1707 CO^2:95.7% Ar:2.5% N^2:1.2% O^2:0.56% CO:0.04%

‘My wits begin to turn.’ – King Lear

W N 3FT

SOL:1707 CO²:95.7% Ar:2.5% N²:1.2% O²:0.56% CO:0.04%
the overloaded ark
W N 3FT
PAGE:71

‘gravity begins at home, my brother’ – Ivor Cutler

(nice dream)

The poet is listening
to her headphones
again, mapping the dust

– green fields and willow groves –

her wanderlust
is a way of hearing ghosts
old dialect words
lost to shoals
a reversal of process

herring, turtle, sandwich, egg-meat

'your field-mice are my words' she whispers

SOL:1707 CO^2:95.7% Ar:2.5% N^2:1.2% O^2:0.56% CO:0.04%

01100010 01101001 01100111 00100000 01110011 01110000 01100001 01100011 01100101 00100000 01100010
01101001 01100111 00100000 01110100 01101001 01101101 01100101 01100010 01101001 01100111 00100000
big space
01110011 01110000 01100001 01100011 01100101 01100010 01101001 01100111 00100000 01110100
01101001 01101101 01100101 01100010 01101001 big time 00100000 01110011 01110000 01100001 01100011
01100101 00100000 01100010 01101001 01100111 00100000 01110100 01101001 01101101 01100101 01100010
big space
01101001 01100111 00100000 01110011 01110000 01100001 01100011 01100101 00100000 01100010 01101001
01100111 00100000 01110100 01101001 01101101 big time 01100010 01101001 01100111 00100000 01110011
01110000 01100001 01100011 01100101 00100000 01101001 01100111 00100000 01110100 01101001
big space
01101101 01100101 01100010 01101001 01100111 00100000 01110011 01110000 01100001 01100011 01100101
big time
00100000 01100010 01101001 01100111 00100000 01101001 01101101 01100101 01100010 01101001
01100111 00100000 01110011 01110000 01100001 big space 01100101 00100000 01100010 01101001 01100111
00100000 01110100 01101001 01101101 01100101 01100010 01101001 01100111 00100000 01110011 01110000
big time
01100001 01100011 01100101 00100000 01100010 01101001 01100111 00100000 01110100 01101001 01101101
01100101 01100010 01101001 01100111 00100000 big space 01110000 01100001 01100011 01100101 00100000
01100010 01101001 01100111 00100000 01110100 01101001 01101101 01100101 01100010 01101001 01100111
big time
00100000 01110011 01110000 01100001 01100011 01100101 00100000 01100010 01101001 01100111 00100000
01110100 01101001 01101101 01100101 01100010 big space 01100111 00100000 01110011 01110000 01100001
01100011 01100101 00100000 01100010 01101001 00100000 01110100 01101001 01101101 01100101
big time
01100010 01101001 01100111 00100000 01110011 01110000 01100001 01100011 01100101 00100000 01100010
01101001 01100111 00100000 01110100 01101001 01100101 01100010 01101001 01100111 00100000
big space
01110011 01110000 01100001 01100011 01100101 01100010 01101001 01100111 00100000 01110100
big time
01101001 01101101 01100101 01100010 01101001 01100111 00100000 01110011 01110000 01100001 01100011
01100101 00100000 01100010 01101001 01100111 01110100 01101001 01101101 01100101 01100010
big space
01101001 01100111 00100000 01110011 01110000 big time 01100011 01100101 00100000 01100010 01101001
01100111 00100000 01110100 01101001 01101101 01100101 01100010 01101001 01100111 00100000 01110011
big space
01110000 01100001 01100011 01100101 00100000 01101001 01100111 00100000 01110100 01101001
01101101 01100101 01100010 01101001 01100111 big time 01110011 01110000 01100001 01100011 01100101
00100000 01100010 01101001 01100111 00100000 01110100 01101001 01101101 01100101 01100010 01101001
big space
01100111 00100000 01110011 01110000 01100001 01100011 01100101 00100000 01100010 01101001 01100111
00100000 01110100 01101001 01101101 01100101 big time 01101001 01100111 00100000 01110011 01110000
01100001 01100011 01100101 00100000 01100010 01101001 01100111 00100000 01110100 01101001 01101101
big space
01100101 01100010 01101001 01100111 00100000 01110011 01110000 01100001 01100011 01100101 00100000
big time
01100010 01101001 01100111 00100000 01110100 01101101 01100101 01100010 01101001 01100111
00100000 01110011 01110000 01100001 01100011 big space 00100000 01100010 01101001 01100111 00100000
01110100 01101001 01101101 01100101 01100010 01101001 01100111 00100000 01110011 01110000 01100001
big time
01100011 01100101 00100000 01100010 01101001 00100000 01110100 01101001 01101101 01100101
01100010 01101001 01100111 00100000 01110011 big space 01100001 01100011 01100101 00100000 01100010
01101001 01100111 00100000 01110100 01101001 01101101 01100101 01100010 01101001 01100111 00100000
big time
01110011 01110000 01100001 01100011 01100101 01100010 01101001 01100111 00100000 01110100
01101001 01101101 01100101

W N 3FT

01010011 01100011 01100001 01110010 01100011 01101001 01110100 01111001 00100000 01101001

Scarcity is a bold gesture. Scarcity is bold gesture. Scarcity is a bold gesture. Scarcity is a
bold gesture. Scarcity is a bold gesture. Scarcity is a bold gesture. Scarcity is a bold gesture.
Scarcity is a bold gesture. Scarcity is a bold gesture. Scarcity is a bold gesture. is a bold gesture.
Scarcity is a bold gesture. is a bold gesture. Scarcity is a bold gesture. Scarcity is a bold gesture.
Scarcity is a bold gesture. Scarcity is a bold gesture. Scarcity is a bold gesture. Scarcity is a
bold gesture. Scarcity is a bold gesture. is a bold gesture. Scarcity is a bold gesture. Scarcity is
a bold gesture. Scarcity is a bold gesture. Scarcity is a bold gesture. Scarcity is a bold gesture.
Scarcity is a bold gesture. Scarcity is a bold gesture. Scarcity is a bold gesture. Scarcity is a
bold gesture. Scarcity is a bold gesture. Scarcity is a bold gesture. Scarcity is a bold gesture.
Scarcity is a bold gesture. Scarcity is a bold gesture. Scarcity is a bold gesture. Scarcity is a
bold gesture. Scarcity is a bold gesture. Scarcity is a bold gesture. Scarcity is a bold gesture.
Scarcity is a bold gesture. Scarcity is a bold gesture. Scarcity is a bold gesture. Scarcity is a
bold gesture. Scarcity is a bold gesture. Scarcity is a bold gesture. Scarcity is a bold gesture.
Scarcity is a bold gesture. Scarcity is a bold gesture. Scarcity is a bold gesture. Scarcity is a
bold gesture. Scarcity is a bold gesture. Scarcity is a bold gesture. Scarcity is a bold gesture.
Scarcity is a bold gesture. Scarcity is a bold gesture. Scarcity is a bold gesture. Scarcity is a
bold gesture. Scarcity is a bold gesture. Scarcity is a bold gesture. Scarcity is a bold gesture.
Scarcity is a bold gesture. Scarcity is a bold gesture. Scarcity is a bold gesture. Scarcity is a
bold gesture. Scarcity is a bold gesture. Scarcity is a bold gesture. Scarcity is a bold gesture.
Scarcity is a bold gesture. Scarcity is a bold gesture. Scarcity is a bold gesture. Scarcity is a
bold gesture. Scarcity is a bold gesture. Scarcity is a bold gesture. Scarcity is a bold gesture.
Scarcity is a bold gesture. Scarcity is a bold gesture. Scarcity is a bold gesture. Scarcity is a
bold gesture. Scarcity is a bold gesture. Scarcity is a bold gesture. Scarcity is a bold gesture.
Scarcity is a bold gesture. Scarcity is a bold gesture. Scarcity is a bold gesture. Scarcity is a
bold gesture. Scarcity is a bold gesture. Scarcity is a bold gesture. Scarcity is a bold gesture.
Scarcity is a bold gesture. Scarcity is a bold gesture. Scarcity is a bold gesture. Scarcity is a
bold gesture. Scarcity is a bold gesture. Scarcity is a bold gesture. Scarcity is a bold gesture.
Scarcity is a bold gesture. Scarcity is a bold gesture. Scarcity is a bold gesture. Scarcity is a
bold gesture. Scarcity is a bold gesture. Scarcity is a bold gesture. Scarcity is a bold gesture.
Scarcity is a bold gesture. Scarcity is a bold gesture. Scarcity is a bold gesture. Scarcity is a
bold gesture. Scarcity is a bold gesture. Scarcity is a bold gesture. Scarcity is a bold gesture.

00100000 01101001 01110011 00100000 01100001 00100000 01100010 01101111 01101100 01100100

Opportunity's maker

a young woman, a child, an artist,
a bowl of fruit, a light box, a tree-climber
called Grace knits an Adam
and an Eve from string
a search engine suggests
the seven-year old
use Meccano to engineer
a structure
able to propel
the couple
into outer space

still

she doesn't understand

the underlying mechanism
of desire

Why is space outside? Shall we let him in? Opportunity asks Mario-bot

'Space isn't something
that happens
beyond the ionosphere. We
are in space

right now' – Timothy Morton

SOL:1707 CO^2:95.7% Ar:2.5% N^2:1.2% O^2:0.56% CO:0.04%

a wake of poets silently

murder

poet, artist, rover, identity crisis

Mornington Crescent!

cup of tea?

the cadavers are still stuck on the Central line

the vultures circle on the underground

a swirl of ice cream

melting lakes

a cow's udder

a Carpathian mountain range – why wait?

3FT W N

Curiosity sings
into Spirit’s radio transmitter

…

Grace, the Ventriloquist

Adam:

there's no point looking back we'll never mend
this wound

Eve:

mind the gap

their sins make Grace
laugh and grace
like earth is only

Opportunity's Last Moments

silk silken silk silk silken silk silk silken silk silk silken silk silk silken silk silk silken silk
silk silken silk silk silken silk silk silken silk silk silken silk silk silken silk silk silken silk
silk silken silk silk silken silk silk silken silk silk silken silk silk silken silk silk silken silk
silk silken silk silk silken silk silk silken silk silk silken silk silk silken silk silk silken silk
silk silken silk silk silken silk silk silken silk silk silken silk silk silken silk silk silken silk
silk silken silk silk silken silk silk silken silk silk silken silk silk silken silk silk silken silk
silk silken silk silk silken silk silk silken silk silk silken silk silk silken silk silk silken silk

Ω Ω Ω

silk silken silk silk silken silk silk silken silk silk silken silk silk silken silk silk silken silk
silk silken silk silk silken silk silk silken silk silk silken silk silk silken silk silk silken silk
silk silken silk silk silken silk silk silken silk silk silken silk silk silken silk silk silken silk
silk silken silk silk silken silk silk silken silk silk silken silk silk silken silk silk silken silk
silk silken silk silk silken silk silk silken silk silk silken silk silk silken silk silk silken silk
silk silken silk silk silken silk silk silken silk silk silken silk silk silken silk silk silken silk
silk silken silk silk silken silk silk silken silk silk silken silk silk silken silk silk silken silk

a cut ribbon

'I am thinking today of that beautiful
land I shall reach when the sun go-eth
down. Will there be any stars
in my crown? When at evening
the sun goe-eth down? When I wake
with the blest in mansions of rest,

will there be any stars in my crown?'

– 'Will there be any stars?' *Heavenly Highway Hymns*

SOL:1707
CO^2:95.7%
Ar:2.5%
N^2:1.2%
O^2:0.56%
CO:0.04%
'My battery is low and it's getting dark'
PAGE:87
3FT W
N

www.ingramcontent.com/pod-product-compliance
Lightning Source LLC
Chambersburg PA
CBHW060932170426
43193CB00027B/3000
* 9 7 8 1 9 1 2 2 1 1 4 4 9 *